I0925735

Teach Your Child the ABCs of How to Become Rich
"A Step-by-Step Approach"

Lemar McNair

Outskirts Press, Inc.
Denver, Colorado

Outskirts Press
http://www.outskirtspress.com

ISBN-10: 1-4327-0419-2
ISBN-13: 978-1-4327-0419-3

Outskirts Press and the "OP" logo are trademarks belonging to Outskirts Press, Inc.

Printed in the United States of America

Table of Contents

Introduction

The purpose of this self-help book is to show parents how to prepare their child for riches from the embryonic stage of life to college graduation. "Rich" refers to the overall development of the child in the areas of living a healthy lifestyle, handling financial matters, pursuing the spiritual presence of God, and achieving educational excellence. This book is a didactic tool for parents to use. The title, *A Step-by-Step Approach – Teach Your Child the ABCs of How to Become Rich,* cites the Word of God throughout, as it is the foundation of this book. Parents will be able to teach their children the principles stated in this book and implement them in their parental roles.

Foreword

In October 2006, I received a call from my daughter informing me that she was pregnant. I remember that countless thoughts ran through my mind at that moment, with the primary one being that her child—my grandchild—be healthy, with ten fingers and toes, and be enveloped in love. After the initial shock wore off, I began to think about my daughter's health, wondering if she would do what would be required of her in order for her child to have a healthy head start in life—eating healthy, taking prenatal vitamins, being under the care of an obstetrician or gynecologist from the inception of her pregnancy up to delivery, etc. Her doing all of these things and providing love and a solid foundation for her child were essential.

My thoughts then shifted to my other grandchildren's futures—the cost of private schools and college tuition. How would my son and daughter be able to prepare for these expenses? I later recounted this scenario to a friend who inquired about my great-grandfather and asked what his first name was. "I don't know," I told him. "Why?", he replied, as if to say, "How could you not know your great-grandfather's first name?" He then asked me who John D. Rockefeller was, and I told him about the oil tycoon and real estate magnate. He said, "You know the first name of someone else's great-grandfather, but you don't know your own."

It finally dawned on me that my great-grandfather had not left a legacy or trust fund for me to know him by. Then the same friend asked, "Do you believe in the promises of God?"

"Of course," I replied. He pointed out that the Jewish believers represent two percent of the world's population and forty-five percent of the top entrepreneurs featured in *Forbes 400 Richest Americans*. He then stated that the Jewish people definitely believe in God and are living on His promises. He went on to suggest that while Christians believe in the promises of God, it is possible that some of Christ's followers do not see the tangible manifestations of His promises, nor live an abundant life as He promised because they do not expect His riches to be bestowed upon them.

This conversation prompted me to delve into some in-depth research to determine the overall upbringing of those who are rich in financial, spiritual, health, and educational matters. How did they handle rejection? What was their relationship with God? What was their lifestyle regarding health? Typically, what were their lives like from childhood into adolescence and then on to adulthood before they struck it rich? How were they nurtured while in their mothers' wombs? How were they reared? With siblings or as an only child? How did they behave socially in school? Did they get along well with their peers and teachers? What career paths did they choose?

As I discussed these thoughts with my friend, Tina, who is a consultant, she told me about the educational training program she sponsors every year. The focus of this program is teaching kids how to manage their finances responsibly and learn about becoming entrepreneurs so that they can be in business for themselves instead of having to work for someone else.

This discussion prompted us to discuss various "what-if" scenarios that eventually led to the writing of a book—a didactic tool for parents. The title, *Teach Your Child the ABCs of How to Become Rich,* cites the Word of God throughout as it is the book's foundation. It is because of God that we live and move. God does, indeed, want every Christian to experience a life full of joy and happiness.

The purpose of this book is for parents to teach their children the principles stated in the book and implement them in their parental roles in an effort to bring up their child in a way that is, and will continue to be, most beneficial to and for them. Proverbs 22:6 admonishes parents to "train a child in the way he should go, and when he is old, he will not turn from it." The parents will benefit directly because they will learn vital lessons that will assist them in their quest to secure spiritual, educational, healthy, and material wealth. Children will see that having money, nice cars, and houses is not bad and that, in fact, the Lord wants us to achieve success. However, the love of money is the root of all evil, so says I Timothy 6:10. The Word of the Lord speaks for itself, so there is nothing wrong with parents showing their children how to obtain wealth as long as the roadmap to becoming rich—emotionally, mentally, healthily, and in the material sense—is obtained God's way and is supported by the Holy Scriptures rather than by the way of the world. A board game is also being designed to illustrate the same principle. The book and board game go hand in hand because the game will reinforce for both the parents and the children what they read and what was read to them.

Studies have proven that children learn by repetition. The board game will provide this, while simultaneously being a fun pastime for children. Reinforcing the steps outlined in this book will ensure great success, not in the way of the world, but in God's way! Sit down, gather your family around, and read these principles one by one and get these awesome instructions into your spirit. Then begin to meditate and implement these principles. Begin to call those things that are not as though they were as the Bible instructs. May this book bless you and your family.

Contact me via email at <u>lemar.mcnair@sbcglobal.net</u> if you have any questions or would like to arrange a speaking engagement with a book signing.

Please visit the website <u>www.kidrich.biz</u> to obtain other valuable information and to download the CD single soundtrack for the book.

Acknowlegments

First, I would like to acknowledge Jesus as my Savior because He died for me so that I may have eternal life. To my lovely wife, Linda McNair through your encouragement, I have come to have a relationship with Christ. To Holly Fowlkes who lent her time and skill to assist me in refining *Teach Your Child the ABCs of How to Become Rich* so that your and your children's lives will be changed for the better. To my daughter and her husband, Callie and Henry Butler. The birth of their child has inspired me to write this book as a tool to be used by parents and grandparents as they teach their children. To my son and his wife, D'Antonio and Michela Wilson, who have produced beautiful children who will be able to benefit from the instructions in this book. To Cliff and Yolanda Magee who have recently united in marriage and are starting a new family. To Melissa Magee who is exceptional and special. The sky is the limit and may you be blessed with continued success. To my grandchildren, Sage Magee and Taylor Nelson, and godson, Malik Chavers, who have helped me perfect certain aspects of this book by imparting their wisdom and insight in designing the board game. To the other grandkids: Lil Dee, Lil Cliff, Mackenzie, Icyion, and DJ, who are now young but will still have the opportunity to learn various aspects of this book and improve their lifestyle. To my parents, Lemar and Henrietta McNair, who have always instilled in me throughout my life that I can do anything with God's help. Special thanks, also, to my pastor,

Frank Wilson, who has encouraged me to read a chapter of Proverbs every day for the rest of my life so that I can be filled with wisdom and knowledge. To my sister and brother-in-law, Eli and Hedy Walls, who have introduced me to people with whom I have consulted in the development of this book. I pray for continued success for their children, Lisa, Kenyatta, Sarah, Nicole, and Alphonse. To my New Dawn Christian Church family and prayer partners for providing fellowship and encouraging me in my spiritual walk.

To the praise and worship group Soldiers, lead by Billy Davis Jr. and Marilyn McCoo, for creating a spiritual platform to allow Christians to give their testimony for what the Lord is doing in their lives. To all of my family, friends, and associates who have contributed to my life in one way or another.

Chapter 1:
The Genius Inside

Every baby is born to learn

In fact, infants are like tiny sponges and are designed by God, Elohim the Creator, to absorb everything. The development of intelligence actually begins in the womb. Therefore, it is imperative for the mother to live a healthy lifestyle in order to protect and nourish the unborn child. Researchers have noted that the fetus experiences the most prenatal brain growth between weeks 20 through 25 and that choline is a nutrient that helps stimulate learning. Excellent sources of choline are beef, fish, soy, and eggs. "According to a recent follow-up study published in *Pediatrics*, decosahexaenoic acid—also referred to as DHA—and an Omega-3 fatty acid, found in fish, also play an important role in fetal brain development, visual function, and the rate at which the brain processes information."[1] In the initial study, pregnant women were chosen randomly to receive two teaspoons a day of either cod-liver or corn oil beginning in the eighteenth week of their pregnancies and continuing until three months after delivery. When the children reached four years of age, they received a standardized intelligence test. The children whose mothers had taken cod-liver oil scored significantly higher than those whose mothers had taken corn oil.

Discussing the benefits of DHA with one's physician is recommended. Good dietary sources of Omega-3 fatty acids and DHA include:

- Fish and all seafood
- Vegetable oils such as flaxseed, soy, peanut, and canola oils
- Dry fruits, such as walnuts and almonds
- Kidney beans, avocados, fenugreek seeds, etc.

DHA from vegetarian sources, such as marine algae, is better than fish oil capsules, especially during pregnancy.

Healthy and smart babies are essential

Having healthy and smart babies is a requirement every mother would want, so the following must be considered:

- Eating healthy food – Remember the old adage, "You're eating for two." With this in mind, make nutrient-rich, not caloric-rich, choices. Say "yes" to 75-100 grams of protein, organic fruits, vegetables, beans, lentils, asparagus, spinach, nuts, and free-range and antibiotic-free animals. Say "no" to sugar and its substitutes, wheat, dairy, and hydrogenated fats. Say "once in a while" to small, cold-water fish and soy products. Take the time to sit down and eat slowly and chew your food well before swallowing it.

- Watching what you drink – Drink at least eight cups of good-quality water that is free of such minerals as sulphur. No alcohol, sodas (especially diet), caffeinated teas or coffees.

- Deep relaxation and sleep – Learn to meditate, take a yoga class for expectant mothers, and practice breathing deeply every day. Oxygenation of cells enhances their function, allowing blood to flow more freely. Releasing stress gives the woman's body an opportunity to direct its energy toward growing a healthy baby. Go to bed before

10:00 p.m. and get at least nine hours of sleep.

• Exercise – Stretch to increase flexibility. Walk or attend a class such as Pilates two or three times a week.

• Avoiding toxic exposures – Now is not the time to paint the baby's room, lay new carpet, or spray for termites. Spruce up the house only with "green" products, such as non-toxic and bio-based cleaners. Avoid using chemicals, pesticides, textiles, beauty products, or having any radiation performed, unless directed by a physician, as these things will be harmful to both mother and your developing child. No vaccines with thimerosal, which is a mercury-containing organic compound, including flu shots, should be administered. Use organic cosmetics. Your being conscientious during your pregnancy will pay off.

Read the Bible-one chapter of Proverbs daily

It is imperative that all bases be covered for the expectant mother and it is suggested that the mother read a Bible chapter in Proverbs once daily during her pregnancy. The Book of Solomon in the Bible was named after its author—Solomon himself. He was born around 974 B.C and was installed as King of Israel by his father, David. Solomon was terrified of ruling Israel, fearing that he did not have the wisdom to do so. God appeared to him and asked him what he wanted, and Solomon responded by asking only for wisdom and knowledge.

As a mother responsible for another life, you, too, must exercise your God-given wisdom in rearing your little one. The Lord commands us in Proverbs 4:7 to be wise: "Wisdom is supreme; therefore, get wisdom. Though it cost all you have, get understanding." Have faith and trust in God and instill good, positive things into your child's life. When you do this regularly, your child will be one of the few to achieve incredible outcomes because you took the lead by giving him or her a head start. Solomon's wisdom, success, and wealth increased beyond imagination because he obeyed the Lord. The Book of Proverbs contains many of Solomon's laws for living life wisely.

Program your child

In an *Essence* magazine article of July 1991, Loretta Dabbs wrote, "It may sound manipulative, but I programmed Lisa, my only child, to be an independent thinker. By placing emphasis on certain values, we all program our children in one way or another. For example, our young ones accept our religious preferences and internalize both our positive and negative attitudes toward the opposite sex. And all too often, girls are programmed to think with their hearts rather than their heads. But a time when being 'feminine' is only part of the equation for becoming a successful woman, we must teach our daughters to think logically and strategically."[2] The bottom line is that your first opportunity to program your child is when the fetus is in the womb. Why not start at the beginning to ensure that he or she enters into the world with the best possible chance to achieve greatness? You will be able to "speak life" into your child at the infancy stage. Ask yourself, "What do I have to lose by following these steps?" The answer is simple. You have nothing to lose and everything to gain because your child will benefit from your choice to be proactive and forward thinking about his or her future. The choice is yours, so step out on faith, trust in God, and watch the miracles of God unfold.

Action Steps

Proverbs 5:7 (NIV)
"Now then, my sons, listen to me; do not turn aside from
what I say"

1. Teach your baby while in the womb
2. Eat well-balanced meals
3. Live a healthy lifestyle
4. Exercise regularly
5. Get plenty of rest
6. Meditate daily on the Book of Proverbs because it gives insight on how to live wisely
7. Avoid exposure to toxic products

Chapter 2:
Got Milk?

Proverbs 1:8-9 (NIV)
"Listen, my son, to your father's instruction and do not
forsake your mother's teaching
They will be a garland to grace your head and a chain to
adorn your neck"

Babies can learn

Research indicates that babies learn more in their first
three years of life than at any other time. Your baby is like
a sponge and will literally absorb what he or she sees, feels,
tastes, touches, and hears. Therefore, you must create a
stimulating environment for your baby. Doing this will
create an environment conducive to learning. One of the
most important things a mother can do is talk to her baby.
This will allow the child to become an excellent
communicator. As human beings we learn by repetition.
Communication is a vital tool and is an imperative key to
success. Good communication skills will help a child excel
in school and live a successful life.

It is extremely important that you speak slowly and
clearly so that your baby can differentiate one sound from
another. In addition, allow your child to watch your facial
expressions as you talk so he or she can visualize the
specific process of how to form his or her mouth when
making various sounds. Place different colored objects
within your child's view and read and name the objects and
their colors. Speak simply and always call your baby by his
or her first name. You should always use gestures as you

talk and make eye-to-eye contact with your baby. This makes the interaction between mother and baby more intimate. You will be able to capture and hold your baby's attention by moving your eyes and mouth. Use inflection as you change the pitch of your voice and determine which one your baby responds to the most. Whichever level gets the most smiles is surely the winner.

Read to your child daily
The second most important thing that will enhance your child's communication skills is to read to your child several times a day. This will create a bonding time. Place the baby in your lap while sitting in a comfortable chair and make sure that the book you select has plenty of pictures. Point to the picture as you describe what you see. Change the tone and pitch of your voice and make eye contact with your child as you touch his or her face, toes, fingers, etc. These special, intimate moments also create great opportunities to sing to your baby by connecting the words in the picture book with a rhythmic tune or a nursery rhyme. Incorporate the use of soft, plush toys into your reading time by shaking a rattler, touching your baby's face, hands, and stomach, etc. It never hurts to allow your baby to listen to soft music or tapes that encourage early-stage learning. Research has shown that your baby will not become any smarter if he listens to classical music. The "Mozart Effect" was first featured in a study done by researchers at The University of California at Irvine in 1993. Recent studies do not support the popular belief that a child will become smarter by listening to classical music. However, it is believed that listening to a Mozart sonata can ignite the brain to tackle mathematical tasks—the science of numbers—because of Mozart's love for math. *American Scientist Online* reports in "Did Mozart Use the Golden Section?" by Mike Kay that

Mozart's sister, Wolfgang, says that her brother "talked or thought of nothing but figures"₃ during his school days. Reportedly, Mozart jotted down mathematical equations in the margins of some of his compositions.

Breastfeeding your baby is healthy
Studies reveal that one of the most significant benefits of breastfeeding your baby is that it enhances brain development and intelligence. In addition, breast milk is the almost-perfect food for newborns as it is sterile, easily digested, non-allergenic, and transmits maternal antibodies that protect babies against many infections and illnesses. Breastfeeding will also create an unforgettable bond between mother and baby.

Healthy eating habits are essential
After the breastfeeding stage, it is of utmost importance to develop healthy eating habits for your baby to imitate as he or she graduates to each stage of eating. At four to six months, your child will be eating single-ingredient foods such as rice, cereal, and processed foods. At seven to eight months, your child will have arrived at Stage 2, which includes feeding your child a diet of strained single-ingredient combination foods such as Gerber peas or carrots. Stage 3 is for nine-to-twelve-month-olds. Small chunks of food are permitted and encouraged to promote "chewing." Serving sizes at this stage are geared to your baby's growing appetite. Stage 4 is for first-year eaters and table food is permitted. During this stage your child can enjoy the same food you do.

Having said this, the mother should develop an eating plan with her doctor to determine what is best for the baby. Your child's eating plan should be tailored specifically to him or her in order to maintain a healthful regimen. Feed your child fresh and natural foods. Good eating habits will ensure that your child will avoid obesity and develop a healthy immune system. Encourage your child to drink water after completing each meal and throughout the day. Make sure the meals you prepare include a variety of foods and that they are well balanced. The four major food groups are grains, vegetables, fruits, and proteins. Consult with your physician regarding the specific types of food in the various food groups that are best for your child based upon his or her age. There are several food groups you definitely want to avoid: foods high in nitrates, those that may present a choking hazard, honey, corn syrup, sugar, salt, and caffeine. The above regimen will create a solid foundation for healthy eating for your child, and when he or she grows up, the good eating habits you helped develop will remain a part of the way of life to which he or she is accustomed.

Pray over your child

Proverbs 22:6 supports this: "Train a child in the way he should go, and when he is old he will not turn from it." Your child is a gift from God and is destined for greatness! Always pray over your child daily and speak positive thoughts into his or her life. God has had a purpose and plan for your child's life even before his or her birth. God had a plan for Moses when he was a baby, and He directed him to lead the people of Israel out of Egypt and into the Promised Land. Do not take God's calling on your child's life lightly!

Develop a healthy learning environment

Keep in mind that every successful and wealthy person started out as a baby, which is the point from which your child is starting. To ensure that your child is rich in every

9

area of his or her life, create an environment that enhances your child's learning experiences. Set aside the required quality time to make a positive impact on your child's future. You are the key that will allow greatness to be unleashed in his or her life. Take the responsibility of raising your child by being actively involved twenty-four hours a day, seven days a week. Do not leave your parental responsibility to television shows, video games and commercials or to other people, as parents are solely responsible for their children's lives.

Action Steps

Proverbs 2:6 (NIV)
"For the LORD gives wisdom; from his mouth come
knowledge and understanding."

1. Talk to your baby
2. Read to your baby
3. Play soft music to your baby
4. Breastfeed your baby
5. Establish good eating habits
6. Give your baby water daily
7. Pray over your baby daily
8. Create a healthy environment for your baby
9. Take responsibility for raising your baby

Chapter 3:
The Toddler

Proverbs 8:32 (NIV)
"Now therefore, listen to me, my children, For blessed are
those who keep my ways."

A new world of learning

Your child is now a year old and is making the
transition from baby to toddler. A new world is about to
open up, one where he or she will be eager to learn and
experience new things. The child's five senses are activated
and he or she is ready to become another explorer like
Christopher Columbus. The road to success begins right
here! It is crucial for your child to be healthy, to feel loved,
and to be involved in an educational, safe, and comfortable
environment to foster learning. Children are more adept at
learning the sound of language and also from visual
perception—seeing objects that will stimulate their senses.
Therefore, you want to take every opportunity to read to
your child and highlight pictures in the book, pointing to
them as you read. This will enable your child to correlate
what he or she hears and sees. Make reading a game so that
the child can become engaged in the activities associated
with the reading exercise. There will be many opportunities
throughout the day that will have academic implications for
your child as you go about your daily routine. You will
want to capture these moments and identify the learning
experiences in order to teach your child properly. A child's
environment plays a major factor in his or her development,
but doesn't necessarily dictate who he or she will become

in the future. A child can be reared in a low-income area and still become a doctor. A parent should actively choose to participate in and meet his or her child's learning needs. This parental role is key in the positive development of your child.

Make learning fun

One argument for a parent not being as active in the learning process as he or she should be quite often is "There just isn't enough time." As a result, the parent may be inclined to leave the developmental stages of learning up to someone else. Time is precious. The seeds you are planting in the life of your child at this stage will equip him or her with a vast amount of knowledge that will enable your child to reach his or her destiny in life. In teaching your child, make learning fun by turning learning exercises into games and by keeping them light and educational. Embrace the teachable moments. There are eight basic skill areas that, as a parent, you should strive to work on with your child:

a. Social/Emotional skills: which will be the greatest measurements of success in life;

b. Self-esteem: which is crucial in learning anything and everything. One must respect himself or herself in order for someone else to follow suit;

c. Physical skills:

d. Communication skills: listening, speaking, singing, drawing, gesturing;

e. Basic concepts: such as colors, letters, numbers, vocabulary;

f. Categorizing skills: being able to differentiate between similarities and differences;

g. Experiences from which a child can draw: These are perhaps the most important of all as they provide a frame of reference for future learning. The child can reflect on certain experiences and draw lessons learned, helping him or her understand the world better. The more experiences from which a child can draw, the better he or she will understand both learning and the world.

Develop your child's intelligence level

At this juncture of your child's development, it is good to recognize which type of intelligence your child may favor. This will allow you to provide additional learning resources to expand upon that particular strength, while also raising the lower levels of intelligence types higher.

• Word smart -- Journalists, lawyers, and storytellers demonstrate language agility. These people are best at using the written or spoken word in order to communicate;

• Logic smart -- People with a great deal of *logical-mathematical intelligence* are best at reasoning and thinking in terms of cause and effect. Scientists, accountants, and computer programmers generally have this ability;

• Picture smart -- Otherwise known as *spatial intelligence*, this involves thinking in pictures or images. Such individuals are often best at following directions or being able to visualize and draw accurately;

• Music smart -- *Musical intelligence* is the ability to keep time with music, sing in tune, and discern the difference between different musical selections. These people can best perceive and appreciate melodies;

• Body smart -- Individuals with *bodily-kinesthetic intelligence* are best able to control their own movements. This involves not only outdoor sports, but tasks such as sewing and carpentry;

• Person smart -- Such persons have the ability to

respond to, understand, and work with other people. This *inter-personal intelligence* is the gift of being able to see things from other people's perspectives;

- Self-smart -- These people tend to be contemplative and can easily access their own feelings. Those with *intrapersonal intelligence* may be introspective and enjoy meditating;

It is important for you to work with your child to develop all of these intelligence types because the more well rounded he or she is, the more successful they will be in many aspects of his or her life.

Encourage physical activities

It is also important to give your child plenty of opportunities to be physically active. Toddlers learn how their bodies work (and burn off energy) by running, jumping, climbing, and exploring their worlds. You probably do not need to take extra steps to make sure your toddler exercises. Toddlers are so active at that age that they get all the exercise they need, just from going about their normal routines.

Develop good eating habits

Your toddler needs about 1,000 calories a day to meet his needs for growth, energy, and good nutrition. He or she will meet this caloric intake as long as it is divided among three small meals and two snacks a day. Toddlers' eating habits fluctuate and are unpredictable. Your toddler needs balanced servings (toddler portions) from the same four basic nutrition groups that you do:

1. Meat, fish, poultry, and eggs;
2. Dairy products;
3. Fruits and vegetables;
4. Cereal grains, potatoes, rice, breads, and pasta.

15

When planning your child's menu, remember that cholesterol and other healthy fats are very important for his or her normal growth and development. Therefore, do not restrict fats during this period.

Your child is special

Always view your child as someone special God has created and for whom He has great plans. Your child has a great calling on his life. Jeremiah 29:11 reads, "For I know the plans I have for you," declares the LORD, "plans to prosper you and not to harm you, plans to give you hope and a future." Isaiah 44:2 reads, "This is what the LORD says— he who made you, who formed you in the womb, and who will help you: Do not be afraid, O Jacob, my servant, Jeshurun, whom I have chosen."

The Lord is saying to Jacob that he has been hand chosen, and so has your child. As a parent, you must nurture your child's gifts. Read a chapter of Proverbs to your toddler and a children's book Bible story everyday. Think about how God had a calling on Moses' life when he was toddler. Moses had the significant responsibility of leading the children of Israel out of Egypt. Make it a habit to pray for your child daily and teach your child how to pray. Teach your toddler about Jesus and make certain that he or she knows that Jesus loves him or her. This spiritual phase is very important in your toddler's life because it sets foundation for his or her spiritual growth and relationship with God. Dedicate your toddler to God as an infant so that He will watch over and protect your little one and have great things in store for him or her.

Action Steps

Proverbs 5:7 (NIV)
"Therefore hear me now, my children, And do not depart from the words of my mouth."

1. Make sure your child is healthy
2. Create a loving relationship with your child
3. Create an environment for learning
4. Read to your child daily
5. Make learning fun by using teaching activities
6. Teach your child the basic skills
7. Work with your child in the multiple intelligence areas
8. Allow and encourage your child to exercise
9. Ensure that your child eats healthful foods
10. Pray for your child daily
11. Teach your child how to pray

Chapter 4:
The Preschooler

Proverbs 22:6 (NIV)
"Train up a child in the way he should go,
And when he is old he will not depart from it."

Early childhood development
You have now made it through the diaper stages and your child is growing into early childhood. You are noticing certain traits, characteristics, and behaviors and are probably wondering where in the world your child learned them. Your child will begin to open up to a new world. He or she will want to touch, taste, smell, and test things for himself or herself and will learn by observation and imitation. He or she will feel a strong urge to use language as he or she is also struggling to gain inner control while developing these skills. The child will be more independent and will focus more on people outside of the family. The interactions with family and outside people will help shape personalities, ways of thinking, and moving. You should be very selective of the television programs your child watches and the types of people he or she comes in contact with since children are easily influenced. Try to avoid being around people who think and talk negatively because it is easy for your child to pick up these distinctive thought patterns.

Make playtime a learning experience
Your child is making developmental strides and at this stage. Children will learn from the manner in which they

play. They can master skills by learning to use symbols, by increasing their language ability and by learning flexible problem-solving techniques. Playing helps your child make adjustments, become inquisitive, and curiously explore what he or she does not understand. For children, playing promotes a higher level of thinking and allows them to master many skills. Therefore, ensure that your child's playtime is geared toward learning experiences, which should cover the following developmental stages:

a. Physical - walking, running, jumping, standing on tiptoes, catching a ball, hopping on one foot, skipping, dressing themselves, painting, cutting a straight line with scissors, drawing, tying their shoes, etc.

b. Social and Emotional – Praising them for their achievements, learning to share and take turns. They enjoy role playing—being someone who they are not. They want to feel important and worthwhile and enjoy playing with other children. They need to know the rules and the consequences of breaking them, be it punishment or how they are reprimanded, and they need to be encouraged to express their feelings verbally. They should believe in their ability to achieve success, be respectful of others, have a trusting and fearless relationship with their parents and a greater degree of latitude in acting out at home, but with pre-set boundaries. This means that they should be able to be more free and relaxed at home but never disobedient or disrespectful. They should engage in conflict and recover quickly, which will make them develop a "thick skin" in order to be tough. They should develop a desire to achieve and possess self-confidence in their abilities to excel. They should experience that which will allow them to succeed or fail and to try again. They should have high standards and expectations and feel free to discover their talents. They should develop their own personal style, participate in

19

many extracurricular activities, and have their dependency needs met at home by having strong maternal attachments that will make them less vulnerable to peer pressures.

c. Intellectual – They learn best by doing. They communicate their needs, are talkative, and ask a lot of questions. They understand basic numbers, can differentiate basic colors, shapes and sizes, and are developing their reasoning ability. Their attention span is longer and they need a balance between active and quiet play.

d. Language – They should be learning to say what they feel with words instead of using actions such as crying, grabbing, hitting, or biting. They should be able to remember parts of a story and can tell longer stories or fantasies. They should also be able to learn 300 to 2,500 words, name basic colors, recite the days of the week and other time-related words. They should understand when two things are the same or different as well as be familiar with the present, past, and future.

e. Spiritual – They should know about Jesus and that He loves them and about the true meaning of Christmas. They should know about God and learn to have faith and trust in Him. They should know about various Bible stories.

f. Creativity – They should be developing their imagination, their ability to communicate and express his or her feelings and ideas in a creative way. They should participate in playtime, art, music, dance, and storytelling, which will increase their ability to listen, observe, and use his or her imagination. These activities will give your child the opportunity to determine the way in which he or she responds to sound, sight, smell, touch, and the way they feel. A wide range of materials and equipment should be used to encourage your child to explore sound, color, shape, texture, form, and space.

g. Moral – They should be developing senses of

values, determining right from wrong, and developing a sense of equality regarding their attitudes toward people with different values. They will behave in ways that will be rewarded and strive to keep themselves out of trouble.

h. Thought Patterns – They should have the ability to make choices, cooperate with their parents and others, make decisions, and understand the consequences of their actions.

Proper nutrition is essential

Your child's nutrition is important to his or her overall health. Proper nutrition should include eating three meals a day and two nutritious snacks, limiting high-sugar and high-fat foods, eating fruits and vegetables, lean meats, and low-fat dairy products, including three servings of milk, cheese, or yogurt in order to meet their calcium requirements. Following these guidelines can also prevent many medical problems, including obesity, which may lead to diabetes. It will also ensure that your child grows to his full stature and potential.

The best nutritional advice that can be given to help keep your child healthy includes encouraging him or her to:
- Eat a variety of foods;
- Burn calories from the food he or she eats by being physically active;
- Choose a dietary plan that includes plenty of grain products, vegetables, and fruits;
- Choose a diet low in fat and cholesterol;
- Choose a diet moderate in sugars and salt;
- Choose a diet that provides enough calcium and iron to meet their growing bodies' requirements.

Encourage positive communication

What we say and how we say it can have a life-changing impact on your child. Your child is soaking up information

21

like a sponge. How you communicate with him or her is very important. If you maintain positive communication with and encourage your child, you will notice the positive impact your uplifting words can have on your offspring. Proverbs 15:1 states, "A gentle answer turns away wrath, but a harsh word stirs up anger."

If your child does something to make you angry, how would you handle the situation? Will you lose control and begin to scream and speak negative words about your child? How will your child respond to your hurtful outbursts and how will this impact his future behavior?

Proverbs instructs us to impart kind words to our children using a soft and gentle tone when speaking to them and in our teaching approach. You, the adult, will be able to effectively communicate unconditional love to your child, which will be the primary motivator for your child to change his or her inappropriate behavior. "The tongue that brings healing is a tree of life, but a deceitful tongue crushes the spirit," Proverbs 15:4 states.

Encouraging communication improves not only your child's life but also the lives of those around him. When the child's spirit is broken, not only does the relationship suffer but the child can experience emotional scarring that can affect him or her for the remainder of his or her life. You have no idea how much power resides in what you say and how you say it, so choose your words carefully before speaking. Remember, Proverbs 18:21 states, "The tongue has the power of life and death, and those who love it will eat its fruit."

Action Steps

Proverbs 16:23 (NIV)
"The heart of the wise teaches his mouth and adds persuasiveness to his lips."

1. Allow your child to play and learn
2. Monitor television programs
3. Monitor interactions with other people
4. Help your child to develop in the following areas:
    a. Physical
    b. Social / Emotional
    c. Intellectual
    d. Language
    e. Spiritual
    f. Creative
    g. Moral
    h. Thought Patterns
5. Encourage healthy eating habits
6. Speak positive words to your child
7. Pray for your child daily

Chapter 5: Elementary-School Age

Proverbs 20:7 (NIV)
"The godly walk with integrity;   blessed are their children who follow them."

Excellence is a standard

You are now ready to prepare your child for elementary school. First, you want to teach your child to achieve excellence and instill in his or her mind that it is a standard. The standard of excellence must become the expectation that children will have to live up to. Use plenty of love by showing the difference between excellence and mediocrity in the various things that they will accomplish throughout their lives. You can help your child develop these skills by setting an example and providing training in the following areas.

a.   Time management – Give your child a childproof watch with an adjustable, comfortable wristband and teach him or her how to tell time. Conduct various exercises such as asking them to do something at a certain time. This will create a routine. Observe whether or not your child conducts the task on time, before time, or after the fact. Point out to your child that the excellence standard—his or her going "above and beyond"—would be to conduct the desired task before the designated time is up. This time-management exercise can apply to turning in school homework, performing chores around the house, etc. Teach your child the importance of doing more than what is expected of him or her at all times.

b. Resourcefulness – Teach your child about the information age—technology. There are various ways you can do this. An excellent way to multi-task—that is, teaching your child about the information age—is reading and going to the local library. Research certain subjects on the computer. Go to search engines and type in key words to narrow your search. Please monitor your child at all times while he or she is on the computer and be sure to place security restrictions on accessing certain sites that are not child friendly. Equip your child with spelling aids such as a dictionary and teach him or her how to use it effectively. Show your child how and when to properly use the encyclopedia and the thesaurus-a type of dictionary that lists various words that mean the same thing. It is of utmost importance for your child to know how to do research so that he or she can access information.

c. Independent thinking – It is important that your child become an independent thinker. Teach your child how to make decisions. At this stage, children must be taught the difference between right and wrong since consequences will come with every decision that your child will make. They will either be positive or negative and could be helpful or hurtful. The results could impact them immediately or in the future. At this stage of your child's development, you should have already created and implemented an open line of communication whereby the child can talk to you openly and honestly about everything. You should always include role-playing in the decision-making process so that your child can visualize his or her decision in his mind and the consequences of the decision before he or she makes a decision. This could be the key to cutting back on inappropriate behavior. For your child to be able to associate consequences with the corresponding actions or punishments is a sign of growth and maturity. Basic steps in the decision-making process are evaluating the pros, cons, and possible solutions; developing a plan of action; modifying the plan on an as-needed basis; writing down what action he would like to perform and talk to you about. After these steps are followed, you would want your child to perform what-if scenarios before making the decision. Your child will be able to mentally examine the decision in his mind before reaching a conclusion. These steps will teach your child how to become a critical thinker.

    d. Communicator – Being an effective communicator is essential if your child is to achieve excellence. Teach your child how to enunciate words properly by putting emphasis on the proper syllables and craft complete sentences that include a subject, verb, object and possibly, an adjective that describes the noun. In addition, build upon their vocabulary by helping them read well written articles to learn how to develop proper sentence structure. Demonstrate to your child the proper posture (standing erect), proper tone of voice (not whining or using baby talk), and how to sit still and listen attentively. Teach your child how to be polite and respectful to everyone and not judgmental based upon how someone else looks or speaks. Make sure your child knows to always ask questions if he or she does not understand what you are saying and always repeat the instructions to make sure he or she understands your orders.

Teach your child good money habits

    Parents have a responsibility to teach their children the proper foundation about money and how to handle it responsibly. Money is not a bad thing, but when our perspective on money becomes tainted, it is possible to become greedy.

The Bible says in I Timothy 6:10, "For the love of money is the root of all evil: which while some coveted after, they have erred from the faith, and pierced themselves through with many sorrows."

Your child should be taught the value of money and how it is earned by exchanging goods or services. Therefore, I would encourage you to teach your child the following money habits: Give your child specific tasks to perform around the house while giving him or her an opportunity to earn money for these tasks above and beyond any routine duties. Take your child to the bank and open up a savings account so that your child will get in the habit of saving money and steadily watch his or her savings account grow. Ensure that your child deposits his or her weekly earnings and any special monetary gifts in the account. Of course, the savings account will be in your name, with your child's name added as the secondary account holder if your child is not an adult. Instill in your child the value of saving money for the unexpected things that will come up in life and for certain necessities or even desires.

Show your children how to balance their own checkbooks so that they can record all their earnings and expenses. Show them the difference between what is in the checking account for expenses and the money in their savings account for a "rainy" day or for a special toy or purchase, or even for college. Saving ten percent of one's income is always an excellent idea. Encourage your children to follow suit and save ten percent of their allowance or all other money. Balancing their checkbook and comparing the difference between the balances in the savings and checking accounts are excellent ways for children to improve their math skills while helping to secure their future.

To reiterate, it is extremely important to teach children the importance of taking their weekly earnings and giving one-tenth to the Lord to sow seeds in God's Kingdom. Leviticus 27:30 says, "A tithe of everything from the land, whether grain from the soil or fruit from the trees, belongs to the LORD; it is holy to the LORD." Verse 32 reads, "The entire tithe of the herd and flock—every tenth animal that passes under the shepherd's rod—will be holy to the LORD."

Encourage your child to become a tither as the Word of God instructs us to be. If your child does this, he will be blessed. If not, he will be cursed, so says Malachi 3:8-10. "Will a man rob God? Yet you rob me. But you ask, 'How do we rob you? In tithes and offerings. You are under a curse—the whole nation of you—because you are robbing me. Bring the whole tithe into the storehouse, that there may be food in my house. Test me in this, says the LORD Almighty, and see if I will not throw open the floodgates of heaven and pour out so much blessing that you will not have room enough for it."

If you teach your child to be a tither at a young age, he will have no difficulty giving the Lord the money that belongs to Him when he grows up. Show your child how to save money for things that he wants to purchase even though he may not have all of the money when he would like to purchase a particular item. Explain to him or her the value of sharing with others who are less fortunate. An English clergyman and poet, John Donne, (1572-1631) said it best. "No man is an island." Sharing and being involved with others is how the human race survives.

If you have bad money habits and beliefs, please do not teach your child the same habits. Understand the facts about good money habits. Your child will be watching you and, therefore, you need to demonstrate good, responsible spending habits that your child can imitate.

Help your child with career choices

Now is the time to talk to your child about career choices and attending college. Even though your child could change his or her mind later about his profession and/or undergraduate school, it is best to guide him on the correct road toward maximizing his income potential. Again, you want to set high expectations for your child while loving him or her unconditionally. According to current labor statistics, the highest-paid occupations are physicians, airplane pilots, attorneys, security sales, and engineers. Set aside time to introduce your child to these occupations and explain the value each brings to society. Ask a professional who works in each of these fields to become a mentor to your child and allow him or her to shadow them on the job if possible. This will give your child a crash course in what transpires on a day-to-day basis in these occupations and it will enable you to find out what peaks his interest. Other high-paying careers are athletes, entrepreneurs, and entertainers. Breaking into these careers is often a matter of luck—being at the right place at the right time and being spotted by the right person. Your child should be exposed to these careers as well. If you are an entrepreneur, then you should definitely expose your child to your business and share with him or her what being your own boss entails. This would mean talking to your child about how the business works, allowing him or her to perform some function within your operation under supervision for a hands-on experience and discussing intricate details of the day-to-day operation at the dinner table.

Encourage proper eating habits

It is your responsibility to ensure that your child eats properly. If you adhere to the dietary suggested plan in this book, your child will be a high performer and achiever in everything that he or she does, since they must have the proper nutrients for their body. The U.S Department of Agriculture (USDA) recommends using the Food Guide Pyramid (FGP) as a tool for healthful food choices. Some key guidelines include; not exceeding thirty percent of total energy intake from fat and getting less than ten percent from saturated fats. The FGP for children identifies recommended portions of food from grains (six servings), vegetables (three servings), fruit (two servings), milk (two servings), and meat (two servings) and limiting the intake of fats and sweets. Please avoid giving your children junk food such as fast foods, cold drinks, candy, chips, etc.

Read Bible stories to your child

God has placed a special anointing on your child, and he or she is on this earth to serve God's purpose. Continue to read the Bible to your child and let him know how much God loves him or her. God can use your child just like He used "Boy" King Josiah who became the King of Judah when he was only eight years old. Josiah loved God, and God used him to repair the temple in Jerusalem. While the men were working, they found a scroll that was hidden inside the walls. King Josiah called everyone together to read the scroll, which was the Book of Law. After the reading, everyone promised to each other and to God to always obey His laws. Teach your child to have an open mind and to always be open to the will of God and for God to have complete control over his or her life.

Action Steps

Proverbs 20:11 (NIV)
"Even a child is known by his actions, by whether his
conduct is pure and right."

1. Teach your child that excellence is a standard
2. Teach your child time-management skills
3. Teach your child how to be resourceful
4. Teach your child how to be an independent thinker
5. Teach your child effective communication skills
6. Teach your child responsible and wise money habits
7. Help your child to make career choices
8. Provide the proper nutrient-balanced foods for your child
9. Teach your child to be open to the will of God

Chapter 6:
Junior High School Age

Proverbs 23:24 (NIV)
"The father of a righteous man has great joy; he who has a wise son delights in him."

Introduce your child to stock investing

Now you are ready to introduce your child to the world of investing and entrepreneurship. First, we will start with investing. There are three key elements to consider: capital (money); time; and rate of return on investment (percentage of profits or losses). Kids have more spare time than adults; so, in this sense, children seem to already be ahead of the game. Time is a key element in investing. The stock market fluctuates over a period of time, and its trend is that the market will eventually rise again. Kids can benefit from this market fluctuation phenomenon because of their age and their ability to handle erratic swings in the market. You do not need to be rich in order to invest in the stock market. All it takes is a couple of dollars to purchase a "penny stock" and as little as $20 to invest in the New York Stock Exchange (NYSE). When you buy stock, you are buying a portion of a company. Stocks can be purchased through a broker who will charge a commission on the purchase or sale of the stock. In order to diversify your stock portfolio with a small amount of capital, you should purchase a professionally managed mutual fund. Your financial advisor will advise you regarding which stocks to buy and when to sell them. At the end of the year, the mutual fund would have made either a profit or a loss. However, a mutual fund may have more than 100 stocks in its portfolio compared to your buying only one company stock with limited capital. Several keys of investing are: (1) Think long term—a long-term plan will help smooth out the market on a daily/weekly basis, as well as price fluctuation; (2) Diversify – this will allow you not to depend on one market segment. This is why it is beneficial to have mutual funds in your stock portfolio; (3) Dollar-cost average – this will allow you to invest a fixed amount of money in the up-and-down cycle of the market on a regular basis; (4) Re-balance – will allow you to adjust your portfolio annually by replacing dormant stocks with those with a better future outlook.

Take actions to invest in stocks

You will need to do the following in order to expose your child to the world of investing:

a. Subscribe to *Money Magazine* and to *The Wall Street Journal* and have your child read the articles. Explain them to your child in a way that he or she will understand the main idea of the article.
b. Watch television shows such as Bloomberg and CNN with your child.
c. Set up an appointment to meet with a stockbroker and take your child with you. Have the stockbroker explain the process of investing in stocks and mutual funds and to show your child how to read the stock market and mutual funds cost data in the newspaper. You may also want to ask him or her to recommend a stock and a mutual fund to purchase as well as show your child how to track the recommendations on a daily basis.

d. Deposit some funds in the brokerage account on behalf of your child. He or she should have some money saved from the previous years for this investment.

e. Over the next several weeks, work with your child to show him or her how to track the stock and mutual funds on a daily basis and determine the stock-price trend.

f. Once you are comfortable with the stock and mutual fund, return to the stockbroker's office to purchase the stock. If not, then ask the stockbroker to recommend other stocks and mutual funds and repeat steps "e" and "f."

g. Talk with your child regularly about the content in educational television shows such as National Geographic and newspaper articles and magazines. A parent should always want his child to be well informed in every area of his life.

Encourage entrepreneurship

Statistics show that being an entrepreneur increases one's chances of being rich as opposed to someone who is employed by a company. Going to school will give your child the basic skills to be successful, but will not teach him or her how to become an entrepreneur. It is the parent's responsibility to expose the child to the world of entrepreneurship. Yes, your child is in junior high school and is capable of starting a business, and the following steps will show you how to instruct your child to do so:

1. Evaluate your child's strengths. By now, you should be familiar with them. Help your child to identify those areas and record them on paper. The Lord instructs us in Habakkuk 2:2, per the prophet himself, "And the Lord answered me, and said, 'Write the vision, and make *it* plain upon tables, that he may

34

run that readeth it.' "
2. Choose the right business. Provide various options to your child and help him or her explore those business ideas that match his strengths and interests.
3. Develop a simple business plan. It should target the type of business and service it will provide; who the customers are; whether the business will provide a product or a service; how much customers will be charged; what the operating expenses will be; what the profits will be based upon hypothetical situations; how much money is required to start the business; and who your competitors are.
4. Provide money for the start-up business. Now is your opportunity to step up to the plate and provide the initial funds for your child's business. You are an investor now!
5. Provide a room or garage space that can be turned into an office so that your child can launch and manage his or her business.

Failure is a learning experience

This phase of your child's life will introduce both success and failure as at times business will plummet while at other times it will skyrocket. You want your child to understand fully that the only way to fail at something is by giving up. Instill in your child that he or she should never give up and should always persevere through the challenge that he or she faces at that moment. Teach your child not to trust in his own abilities, but to trust and have faith in God! Teach him how to pray so God can lead him and intervene on his behalf. Work with your child to address any negative emotions and replace them with positive thoughts and feelings. Have your child focus on the things that are going right as opposed to those that are not. Your child has the ability to become successful in anything he puts his or her mind to with the help of the Holy Spirit. Make sure that your child devotes his business venture to God and God will bless the business and cause the business to prosper.

Think about college

Your child should start thinking about which college to attend now based upon his or her career choice. It is never too early to start because your child is exceptional and is expected to do great things!

Your child should be trained scholastically and in life skills and be ready to obtain a four-year-academic scholarship. If you stress the importance of an undergraduate education, your child will achieve this goal and may even go on to post-graduate studies. Therefore, he or she will understand and begin thinking about the courses he or she must take in high school, such as the academic standardized and college-entry assessment examinations. The following are some key steps your child can incorporate into his or her college search:

 a. Use the Internet to find what degree programs are offered by the major universities in which your child is interested.

 b. Attend local college fairs that are often hosted at area high schools and obtain information on the requirements for receiving a fully-paid academic scholarship;

 c. Discuss with the guidance counselors any leads they may have on colleges and their respective contacts;

 d. Search for a college that will meet his academic needs and goals;

 e. Narrow your choices to about five colleges;

 f. Visit the college campuses your child is interested in attending in order to narrow down the top picks.

Exercising and good nutrition are essential

Once again, I must stress how critical good nutrition and exercise are. Buy your child a gym membership so that he or she can exercise at the fitness club on a regular basis. Your child is performing at high levels in every area and his or her body will have to be equally as well tuned as his or her mind. Please refrain from giving junk food to your son or daughter and ensure that he or she eats a variety of healthy foods including: vegetables, fruit, bread, cereal, rice and pasta, milk, yogurt, cheese, meat, poultry, fish, dry beans, eggs, nuts, fats and oils.

Trust and have faith in God

After Saul disobeyed God, he asked Samuel to search for a new king for Israel. Samuel met a man named Jessie who had several sons. Samuel selected the youngest of the sons, who was a sheepherder, to become the new King of Israel. His name was David. Samuel anointed David and he was filled with God's power. David rose to the occasion to defeat the Philistine soldier named Goliath. No matter how many Goliaths confront your child, trust and have faith in God that your child, through the power of God, will overcome whatever challenges, disappointments, or setbacks he may encounter in life! Help your child stay focused on God by encouraging him or her to read The Word of God daily. Remind your child of The Lord's Promises which are "yea" and "amen."

Action Steps

Psalm 112:2 (NIV)
"His children will be mighty in the land; the generation of the upright will be blessed."

1. Teach your child about investing in the stock market
2. Encourage your child to read business related books and magazines
3. Allow your child to view business-related and educational television programming
4. Meet with a stockbroker and open an investment account
5. Encourage your child to start his own business
6. Encourage your child to start looking at colleges
7. Ensure your child eats healthful foods
8. Exercise on a regular basis and devise a personal workout plan

Chapter 7:
Senior-High-School Age

Proverbs 1:8 (NIV)
"Listen, my son, to your father's instruction and do not
forsake your mother's teaching."

Preparing for college

Your child is growing up well and has been
accomplishing the objectives set in the previous chapters.
Senior high school is the last critical stage before your child
goes off to college. By now, your child is focused, smart,
knows his career choice, believes, trusts and has faith in
God, and knows that he can accomplish anything he or she
sets as a goal for himself or herself. This chapter will
discuss additional financial necessities your child will need
to know and tuck away in his mind as he sets out on his
path to become rich in every area of his life, both tangible
and intangible, as he secures his or her future. Keep in
mind that you are arming your child with options that will
brighten your child's future and help him or her succeed in
every area of his or her life. Our basic educational system
will teach your child how to become a good employee but
not how to own and operate a business.

Real estate investing

In the previous chapter financial matters were discussed to
better prepare your child for acquiring and managing money.

Now we will discuss other methods of how to use the money that is being earned and is accumulating. The basic concept of real estate investing is to buy low and sell high. Real estate has produced a vast number of wealthy individuals, so the primary objective is to introduce your child to real estate investing. Below are some fundamental steps in the real estate process that you need to review with your child:

    a. Bird-dogging – You and your child canvas the neighborhood looking for vacant homes. If the home is vacant, perhaps the owner may want to sell it. Since a real estate agent may not be involved, it is possible to purchase the home below its market value. Your child can solicit the help of his fellow classmates by spreading the word that he or she will pay a student for the address of every vacant home they find and bring back to him or her. This is an excellent motivator since children can always find a use for money. Hypothetically speaking, your child could now have over 100 students working on commission for him as they scout out vacant properties. This will teach your child how to utilize the resources around him to help him or her accomplish his or her objectives.

    b. Market analysis – Now your child can check the zip code the property is located in and log on to Realtor.com to determine selling prices of houses in the area.

    c. Research – Once your child has the home address, he or she can call the Clerk of Court or tax assessor to find out who owns the property. The Clerk of Court will provide a name and address. Check the phone book for the telephone number and then call the owner while your child listens and ask him or her about selling his home.

d. Property inspection – Let us say the owner is willing to sell the house. Now, you need to set up an appointment with the owner to perform a property inspection. Be sure to obtain a property checklist sheet, which you can download off the Internet, and review it with your child before making the inspection. In addition, you can hire a certified property inspector to go with you and your child to perform a thorough inspection. Be sure to check the square footage, number of bedrooms and bathrooms, and compare this data to the listing data found on Realtor.com to determine the market value of the house. Make a list of all the needed repairs and get a contractor's estimate for making any adjustments.

e. Making the offer – Tell the owner that you are a first-time buyer on your child's behalf. Ask the owner to finance the property for one year using a "bond for deed." Let him know that you will co-sign the loan for your son or daughter and want the terms to be based on a zero down payment since your child has a limited amount of capital. The offer you would make on the property would be the current market value minus the cost of repairs and minus 20% of the home's market value. For example, say the market value is $100,000 and the cost of repairs is $10,000, the offered price should be $100,000 minus $10,000 and minus 20% of $100,000 =$20,000; this equates to a $70,000 offer.

f. Execute a purchase agreement – Sit down with the owner to draft a purchase agreement with the agreed terms. The owner should finance the purchase with a "bond for deed" or a "wrap-around mortgage" if there is a pre-existing mortgage on the property.

g. Close on the loan – Hire a real estate attorney or an escrow company to close the loan.

h. Market the property – The day after the loan's closing, advertise the property in the local newspaper offering a house for sale for below-market value at $95,000. This will give your child a $10,000 profit ($95,000 - $70,000(mortgage) - $10,000 (repairs) - $5,000 (selling expenses) = $10,000).

i. Close on the sale – Again, hire a real estate attorney or escrow company to close the sale.

j. Repeat the previous steps over and over again.

Encourage creativity and innovation

With all of the channels on television, computer games, etc., children often do not use their minds to achieve creativity. In today's world, you want to make sure your child is aware of problematic situations and is finding appropriate solutions, which could result in a new product or service. Therefore, you need to expose your child to the process of inventing a product or service.

1. Encourage your child to find new ways of doing things with his or her newly created product or service.

2. Once the product or service is identified, the child should search the Internet to see if the product already exists and is patented. If so, your child cannot use that particular product or service.

3. Ask your child some basic questions: What makes the product or service unique? How is what you created different from the competitors'? Can you make the product and sell it at a competitive price? What are the benefits of your child's invention to the customer? What needs do you see being fulfilled

after your invention is on the market that were not being filled before? Are there enough customers in your market to make the business beneficial and lucrative? How will you sell the product? This is when you will help your child to find the answers to these questions through diligent and in-depth research.

4. Log on to www.score.gov, click on the home page, local resources, then select your city and state to find the District Office that is closest to you in order to set up an appointment to obtain business counseling service. SCORE, which is a group of retired executives that provides free and confidential small business advice to help build your business from an idea to a start-up success. The service is free. Allow your child to explain the product or service to the SCORE counselor and the benefits to consumers as a result of your child's invention being in the market. The counselor will decide what the next steps are after listening to your child's presentation.

5. Make sure you instill in your child the basic marketing fundamentals: (a) quality – do it better than anyone else; (b) promotion – buyers must know that your product is on the market and, more importantly, that it meets their need(s). This will motivate consumers to purchase your good or service; (c) price – do it cheaper or provide better value; (d) distribution – make the product, good, or service easy to obtain and get repaired.

Be open to be used by God

Before King David dies, he appoints as king, his son, Solomon, who is twelve years old, at the time, with these words: "I go the way of all the earth. You shall be strong, therefore, and show yourself a man and keep the charge of the Lord your God to walk in His ways, to keep His statutes and His commandments and His testimonies. As it is written in the Law of Moses, that you may prosper in all that you do and wherever you turn." (1 King 2:2-3)

Shortly after Solomon is anointed king, God appears to him in a dream, in which He invites Solomon to make a request for himself. Solomon answers, "I am but a small child. Give therefore your servant an understanding heart to judge your people. "His request pleases God who tells him, "Because you have not requested riches and honor but only that which would benefit all the people, I will give you not only an understanding heart like none other before or after you ... but also riches and honor like no other king in your days."(1 Kings 3:7-13)

I cannot stress this enough. Encourage your child to get in the habit of praying for wisdom and understanding. Make sure he continues to read a chapter of Proverbs daily. His ability, wisdom, and success will be enormous!

Action Steps

Proverbs 3:1-2 (NIV)
"My son, do not forget my teaching, but keep my
commands in your heart, for they will prolong your life
many years and bring you prosperity."

1. Teach your child how to invest in real estate
2. Utilize the resources around you
3. Conduct market analysis and research
4. Perform property inspections
5. Learn the art of the real estate transactions
6. Create a product or service to start a business
7. Analyze the product or service by asking a series of questions
8. Contact SCORE for additional assistance
9. Read a chapter of Proverbs daily
10. Ask God for understanding and wisdom

Chapter 8:
College Student

Proverbs 3:21-22 (NIV)
"My son, preserve sound judgment and discernment, do not
let them out of your sight; they will be life for you, an
ornament to grace your neck"

The journey to college
Congratulations! You and your child are entering the
home stretch. By now, your child has acquired a lot of the
basic knowledge for leading a successful life full of
abundance and prosperity in his or her health, body, mind,
and soul. I applaud you for being persistent and being there
with your child through every step of the way during his or
her early life's journey. I know it was not easy, but you
have persevered and because of your level of commitment,
your child has a great future ahead of him or her. However,
there is some additional information that must be shared
before he or she leaves for college.

Watch out for credit cards
There are countless credit card companies preying upon
your child, hoping to coerce him or her to open an account.
Potential creditors will place one, two, or, even, three credit
cards in his or her hand while promising low monthly
payments as a way to establish credit. Remember, credit is
a game. You must demand of your child that he or she will
not sign up for any credit cards. Creditors prey on college
students because they are full-time students and since most
are not working, they will not be able to make timely

payments. This is a disaster waiting to happen and their credit may be damaged for a long time. A few nice purchases are not worth the penalty your child would pay! The interest rates are extremely high and the child could be burdened with excessive credit card debt before he or she even obtains an undergraduate degree. It is highly recommended to monitor your credit report at least twice a year.

Obtaining a college scholarship is a top priority
By working with your child regarding the principles outlined in this book, I am sure your child has secured a scholarship to a college or university, which will provide a financial opportunity.

First, your child should open an Individual Retirement Account (IRA) that allows him the opportunity to invest in mutual funds. Second, allow your child to take out the IRA maximum amount for a college loan so that he can deposit the funds into his IRA. The interest rates on the student loans are very low and will not have to be repaid until your child graduates from college. The amount of interest earned in the mutual fund should be a lot greater than the interest paid on the student loan. This will allow your child to use inexpensive funds for his retirement stock portfolio.

Apply for college grants
If your child is a wage earner and is submitting his income tax and listing himself as a dependent, he may be eligible for additional college funds because of his income. Please ask him or her to make an appointment with his or her college financial aid office to explore all of his or her options. If your child qualifies for grants based upon his annual income, then the grants can be used to offset the college expenses and the remaining funds can be invested.
Conquer the basics in college

47

There are four basic areas your child will face in college: academic, social, financial, and relationships with professors. I am sure that your child is well equipped to handle these areas as a result of the knowledge acquired from reading the previous chapters. However, I will summarize a few points.

    a. Academic – The primary focus is not to loose sight of the goals set forth for college. There will be a tremendous amount of peer pressure and attraction from the opposite sex. Time management skills will be essential in his or her study habits and extra curricular activities.

    b. Social – He or she should choose his friends very carefully. Hopefully, your child's peers will be career minded and have similar goals. At all costs they should avoid negative-thinking people and those with many negative issues. Your child must take control of his or her environment to ensure that it is conducive for learning.

    c. Financial – Statistics have shown that students have a lot of disposable income. Be sure your student keeps a budget and determines its cash flow. College students pay hundreds of dollars per week eating out. If he or she does not know how to cook, this could be a good time to learn and save money on his food budget.

    d. Relationship with Professors – It is vital for the students to establish a good relationship with all of their professors. This will open the door for your child to possibly help some of them with their research. In addition, your child may need references from some of these professors for summer internships, graduate school, and/or employment. Your child's work ethic will precede him or her when he or she ask for letters of recommendation. Professors can assist your child in identifying opportunities and even partner with your child on researching newly created products and services.

Develop your mind

The most important asset your child will have is his mind, so the key to his continuing success is its training and management. Your child must learn to transform negative thoughts into positive beliefs. The mind is like a sponge and it is easy to give in to negative thinking. Any time the internal voice is speaking negatively, your child must replace the negative thoughts with positive ones. He should visualize whatever the situation is as turning out positive and perform the required actions in order to achieve the desired outcome. Your child should approach all homework and tests with the same mindset. However, keep in mind that your child will still need to study.

Stand on the Promises of God

God has given us the Word and the Word of God contains His Promises. The Promises are for all of us- for those that believe that the Lord Jesus Christ is our Savior! God wants us to have an abundant and fulfilling life. It is His desire for you to be rich and have the desires of your heart. Psalm 37:4 states, "Delight thyself also in the Lord; and he shall give thee the desires of thine heart."

God loves you and will bless you

In closing, I would like to leave you with this scripture from Deuteronomy 28:1-6, 8:11-13 (NIV).

"1 And it shall come to pass, if thou shalt hearken diligently unto the voice of the LORD thy God, to observe and to do all his commandments which I command thee this day, that the LORD thy God will set thee on high above all nations of the earth:

2 And all these blessings shall come on thee, and overtake thee, if thou shalt hearken unto the voice of the LORD thy God.

3 Blessed shalt thou be in the city, and blessed shalt thou be in the field.

4 Blessed shall be the fruit of thy body, and the fruit of thy ground, and the fruit of thy cattle, the increase of thy kind, and the flocks of thy sheep.

5 Blessed shall be thy basket and thy store.

6 Blessed shalt thou be when thou comest in, and blessed shalt thou be when thou goest out.

8 The LORD will send a blessing on your barns and on everything you put your hand to. The LORD your God will bless you in the land he is giving you.

9 The LORD will grant you abundant prosperity—in the fruit of your womb, the young of your livestock and the crops of your ground—in the land he swore to your forefathers to give you.

10 The LORD will open the heavens, the storehouse of his bounty, to send rain on your land in season and to bless all the work of your hands. You will lend to many nations but will borrow from none.

11 The LORD will make you the head, not the tail. If you pay attention to the commands of the LORD your God that I give you this day and carefully follow them, you will always be at the top, never at the bottom."

AMEN!

Action Steps

Proverbs 5:1-2 (NIV)
"My son, pay attention to my wisdom, listen well to my words of insight, that you may maintain discretion and your lips may preserve knowledge."

1. Avoid credit cards
2. Establish an IRA funded by student loans
3. Check for available college grants when your child is carrying himself as a dependent on his personal income taxes
4. Focus on academics
5. Encourage your child to choose friends carefully
6. Maintain a financial budget
7. Establish a relationship with each professor
8. Develop and train your mind
9. Understand and obey God's Word

Appendix

A Prayer to Receive Christ

If for any reason you have not received Christ as your personal savior and would like for Christ to enter into your life, you can use the prayer below:

Lord Jesus, I need You. Thank You for dying on the cross for my sins. I open the door of my life and receive You as my Savior and Lord. Thank You for forgiving my sins and giving me eternal life. Take control of the throne of my life. Make me the kind of person You want me to be.

If you just recited this prayer right now, Christ will come into your life as He promised.

Congratulations on joining the family of Christians!!!!!

Endnotes

1 Karyn Maier, "How to Make a Smart Baby," http://www.epregnancy.com.

2 Loretta Dabbs, "Raising 'no-role' girls - mother's account of raising daughter without concern for sex role stereotypes," Esssence, July 1, 1991.

3 American Scientist Online http://www.americanscientist online

Works Cited

Chapter 1
Rao, Kamini, M.D. "Make Sure You Have A Smart Baby. Here's How." www.in.rediff.com, 2005

Chapter 2
Author Uknown, "Health Eating Starts With Good Choices." www.freshbaby.com

Hewlett, Jerrie, "4 Ways to Have a Smart Baby," "Can an Infant Learn to Read" www.preksmarties.com

Sweeney, Danielle, "Classical Music does not a Genius Make." www.babycenter.com

Leonidas, Leo L., M.D., "Try This to Have a Brilliant Baby (Newborn)." www.preksmarties.com

Lannelli, Vincent, M.D., "How to Talk to Your Baby", pediatrics.about.com

Chapter 3
"Raising a Reader", www.kidsource.com

"Helping Your Child Get Ready for School", www.kidsource.com

"Seven Ways for Your Children to Be Smart," www.kidsource.com

"Fish Oil Improves Toddler Learning Skills,"
www.fishoilblog.com

Mascle, Deanna, "When, What, and How to Begin
Teaching Your Preschooler",
www.familyplayandlearn.com

"Stimulating Toddler Learning,"
www.mcesa.k12.mi.us

"Toddler's Diet", American Academy of Pediatrics,
www.medem.com

Chapter 4
Ticknor, Lynne, M.D., "Teaching Children about Money,"
www.bankrate.com

"Ten Principles for Teaching Children about Money,"
www.freemoneyfinance.com, Sept. 11, 2005

Keith, Kimberly L., "Discover and Nuture Your Child's
Learning Strengths," www.childparenting.about.com

Family First Staff, "Giving Your Child the Excellence
Edge," www.familyfirst.net/famlife/excellence.htm

Danes, Sharon M. and Dunrud, Tammy, "Teaching
Children Many Habits for Life,"
www.extension.umn.edu

Chapter 7
Eglehoff, Tom, "How to Determine If There Is A Need For
Your Product," www.smalltownmarketing.com

Kennon, Joshua, "Teach Your Teen Financial Responsibility," www.beginnersinvest.about.com

Wagner, Karen I., "Things All College Freshman Should Know,", www.psu.edu, August 7, 1997

"How to Survive College in 10 Easy Steps,"January 30, 2000, www.cpinions.com

Prayer to Receive Christ
Bill Wright, "Four Spiritual Laws", copyright 2000, Campus Crusade for Christ, Inc.

Printed in the United States
79141LV00002B/4

9 781432 704193